Original title:
The Roots of Everything

Copyright © 2025 Creative Arts Management OÜ
All rights reserved.

Author: Rosalie Bradford
ISBN HARDBACK: 978-1-80581-754-3
ISBN PAPERBACK: 978-1-80581-281-4
ISBN EBOOK: 978-1-80581-754-3

Embers of the Past

In a time when socks would disappear,
Losing one, we'd shed a tear.
The dryer was a monster, you see,
Eating pairs with glee and esprit.

A T-Rex once wore shoes of style,
Oh, the fashion of that ancient mile!
But history laughed, as it often does,
Did they have a closet? Just because!

Heartbeats in the Earth

A worm wobbles, thinking it's cool,
Taking the dirt, like it rules the school.
Yet ants march in precise formations,
Throwing little parties, no reservations!

The earth's a dance floor, far from dull,
With tiny raves, particles in a whirl.
Mole hills are mountains, by their decree,
While we're dealing with gravity's spree!

Beneath the Canopy

Leaves gossip softly about the breeze,
Whispering secrets, with utmost ease.
While squirrels plot their acorn schemes,
Borrowing time with their fluffball dreams.

A raccoon just laughed, hiding a snack,
"Sharing's for fools," he said, and turned back.
But little do they know, as they play,
Tomorrow's feast could simply decay!

Interlaced Realities

In a world where toast could sing,
And jam could dance like a crazy fling.
Mirrors reflect what we don't see,
Like socks that disappear into glee.

Bananas juggle in a fruity quest,
While apples plan their royal fest.
They're crowned with laughter, ripe with cheer,
In our lunchboxes, they're the real pioneers!

Threads of Identity

In a tangled web, we play our part,
Connecting laughter, a quirky art.
With mismatched socks and hair askew,
We stitch our stories, colorful and true.

Each thread a tale of who we are,
With silly faces, we raise the bar.
Jumping through hoops of baked beans,
Identity's a dance with silly routines.

The Bridge Within

A bridge so wobbly, made of cheese,
A trek across it, oh what a tease!
With squirrels as guides and ducks in tow,
We wobble and giggle, our spirits aglow.

Underneath, the river of thoughts so deep,
We hop and twirl, no time for sleep.
Balancing dreams on a roller skate,
Laughter echoes, never too late.

Silent Beginnings

In whispers soft like popcorn's pop,
Hidden giggles at the very top.
A secret world where chuckles bloom,
Curly whoopee cushions fill the room.

Each silent start a punchline waits,
As we juggle pies on cranky plates.
With stifled laughs and playful pranks,
Our shushed beginnings spark the flanks.

Seeds of Tomorrow

Tiny seeds of chuckles we sow,
In garden beds where whoopee cushions blow.
We water them with giggles and glee,
Watch them sprout into a marionette spree!

Dancing daisies with silly faces,
Leapfrog competitions in wide-open spaces.
For tomorrow we'll harvest a laugh or two,
Growing humor like flowers anew.

Timeless Bonds

In the garden, we all play,
With daisies dancing every day.
A bee tells jokes, while flowers laugh,
Oh, nature's quirks! What a chaff!

The worms have parties underground,
Reminding us where fun is found.
With roots entwined in merriment,
Life's secrets shared, time well spent!

Nature's DNA

In the dirt, we're all related,
Each blade of grass? Highly underrated.
A squirrel cracks jokes from a tree,
Claiming it's the best comedy!

The rivers giggle, the mountains cheer,
Creatures chat far and near.
The trees play tag with the breeze,
Life's a laugh, so take it with ease!

The Core of All Things

In every acorn, there's a jest,
Nature's punchlines, truly the best.
A hedgehog winks and rolls away,
Saying, "Spiky hair's in today!"

The sun grins wide, the moon will tease,
While crickets chirp with utmost ease.
From branches high to roots so deep,
Nature's humor makes the world leap!

Veins of Creation

In the soil, jokes are exchanged,
Insects gossip, completely deranged.
A funny vine climbs up a wall,
Telling tales of a summer ball!

The rivers chuckle, the skies will sing,
As bees in hats do their own thing.
With every bloom, a giggle's shared,
Nature's laughter, always prepared!

Entwined Destinies

In a garden of quirks and vines,
The past and the present dance in lines.
Beneath the soil, secrets giggle,
As history chooses to wiggle.

A potato dreams of being a star,
While grandma's sweater tells tales bizarre.
With every spud, a story springs,
In dance of time, the laughter sings.

Wellspring of Dreams

From deep within, a fountain flows,
Where wishes sprout and mischief grows.
With rubber ducks in a wild parade,
They sail on ships that folklore made.

A dandelion whispers soft,
"Pick me up, and fly aloft!"
In fields of giggles, dreams do bloom,
As shadows chuckle, breaking gloom.

Ancestors' Approaches

In dusty books where wisdom snores,
A great aunt's recipe opens doors.
Her biscuits flop like a clown at play,
And leave your taste buds in dismay!

Gramps insists he won a race,
But claims he lost his shoes in space.
With every tale, the laughter grows,
With each retelling, mischief flows.

The Unfolding Tapestry

Each thread a giggle, each knot a jest,
A tapestry woven with stories blessed.
With colors bright and patterns odd,
It tells of antics, and whims abroad.

As a cat unravels the yarn so sweet,
Each tangled tale is a funny feat.
In every loop, a chuckle hides,
While life and laughter take joyous rides.

Remnants of the Ancients

In the dust of a cave, they dance with glee,
Old cavemen's tales, as wild as can be.
With a rock as their mic, they sing out loud,
Even T-Rex joins, he's feeling quite proud.

Pots and pans from times long past,
Their stories are silly, but they meant to last.
A mammoth's strong trunk, a woolly surprise,
They're just like us, with dimples and sighs.

The Silent Symphony

Behind every tree, there's chatter so sly,
Birds play the strings as squirrels pass by.
With rustling leaves as the fluttering beat,
A concert unfolds, with nuts as the treat.

The whispers of roots play a tune soft and low,
Their giggles and murmurs put on quite a show.
Mice tap dance, while ants march in line,
Nature's own band, never needing a sign.

Hidden Histories

Beneath the floorboards, secrets convene,
With cobwebs and memories, a hoard of the keen.
An old shoe from '72, quite the spectacle,
It had many adventures, oh, it was a spectacle!

Dust bunnies whisper of lost toys and cheer,
The great teddy he frets, he's quite the old dear.
A pirate's lost sock, a knight's shiny lure,
In the tales of the past, we all can endure.

Networks Beneath

Underground cables, a party below,
Wires are twisting, putting on a show.
They dance to the rhythm of signals and sound,
In this underground rave, the fun knows no bound.

Roots intertwine like old friends at a bar,
They gossip and giggle, "Hey, did you see that star?"
The networks of life, tangled yet bold,
Spreading joy below, and stories retold.

Forgotten Footfalls

In the garden where weeds dance free,
A gnome giggles under a leafy tree.
He wiggles his toes in the soil below,
Chatting with worms in a wobbly row.

Old trees whisper with stories untold,
Of shoes left behind when the sun turned cold.
Squirrels chuckle as they chase a thought,
While ants debate the crumbs that they've bought.

A donut's shadow rolls on the grass,
While neighbors wonder where all their cash has passed.
But laughter lingers on this sunny day,
In forgotten footfalls that come out to play.

Where Life's Veins Meet

Beneath the sidewalk where pigeons coo,
Are roots knitting tales of the world we brew.
Subway trains rumble like hungry bears,
While folks step lightly past invisible lairs.

The coffee's brewing, oh what a sight!
With beans having dreams of a caffeine flight.
A squirrel, with plans of a nutty heist,
Dramatically plotting, he rolls like a geist.

At the park bench laughs collide and repeat,
Every new friend feels the rhythm of feet.
Where laughter flows and wit finds a door,
Life's veins pulse louder, asking for more.

Portraits of Potential

In a tree's embrace, kids sketch and doodle,
With dreams in their eyes, a creative poodle.
Crayons and giggles intertwine with delight,
As laughter erupts from a paint-splattered fight.

A seedling brags it's the tallest in town,
While daisies gossip, their petals a crown.
They sneak in jokes of the garden's grand fate,
While kids hear the tales of how roots coordinate.

Old benches chuckle with years as their brush,
Elbows nudge softly, in a talkative hush.
A portrait of joy hangs crooked yet bright,
With smiles carved deep, oh what a sight!

The Subterranean Depths

Down in the dirt where the moles have a ball,
They throw tiny parties in a grand earthen hall.
Rats wear top hats, their tails all askew,
While worms read the news of the world from their pews.

Lamp posts flicker, like stars underground,
As roots gossip while they mingle around.
They swap their secrets, so juicy and bold,
In the underbelly, life's stories unfold.

To the surface, the laughter sometimes escapes,
As shadows of creatures put on silly capes.
In subterranean valleys of whimsy and cheer,
Life taps its toes, just to feel the light near!

Beneath the Surface

In the soil, something's brewing,
Dig a bit, and who knows who's chewing.
Worms debate while plants throw shade,
Underground drama, nature's charade.

Roots are ticklish, they wiggle and squirm,
Talking politics, oh, what a term!
Fungi gossip, they share the news,
While sprouting veggies pick and choose.

Whispers of Origins

A potato whispers to a carrot,
"I've got eyes, how about you parrot?"
They giggle together, it's quite absurd,
In the garden, an unspoken word.

Beets bouncing to a funky beat,
Radishes rolling, oh what a feat!
All are plotting their salad fame,
The veggies all want to stake their claim.

Unseen Threads of Life

Fiber threads are weaving tales,
Underfoot, the humor prevails.
A vine whispers jokes to the grass,
While daisies sit, enjoying the sass.

Twisting tales like old grandpas do,
"I'm the tallest," says one, "How 'bout you?"
Petunias giggle, they know the score,
In the tapestry, they spin and explore.

The Germination of Essence

Tiny seeds with big, bold dreams,
Chatting loudly, or so it seems.
"What are we, if not sprouty clowns?"
"Let's take root, and dance in gowns!"

Nature's playground, full of cheer,
Germs of joy, with no fear near.
Sprouts parading in their green hats,
Life's a joke, best shared with chitchats.

Hidden Pathways

In the garden where gnomes hide,
Come and join the little ride.
Digging deep for treasures rare,
We find floppy socks and stale air.

Underneath the kitchen stair,
A secret entrance, shall we dare?
With jelly beans and lollipop stew,
Come on, let's see what we can brew!

Worms do waltzes in the dirt,
While ants wear tiny little shirts.
A misplaced trowel, what a find,
Unraveling mysteries, one of a kind!

So here's to laughter, cheers, and fun,
Chasing shadows, hiding from the sun.
Amid peculiar paths and laughter's might,
Who knew dirt could be such a delight?

Origins of Wonder

Once upon a twisty vine,
A pickle whispered, 'Eat me, I'm divine!'
In pickle jars where dreams reside,
You'll find the secrets we can't abide.

Marshmallow clouds float on by,
While spaghetti trees reach for the sky.
Noodles wiggle and dance all night,
Turning dinner into sheer delight.

Cabbages munch on stories old,
As beetles wear hats made of gold.
In this world where whimsy reigns,
We'll gather giggles in our brains.

From jellybeans to tickling air,
Every oddity is beyond compare.
Savor the magic, take a chance,
For the wonder tales love to dance!

The Heart of What Was

In the attic, dust bunnies play,
With old toys having their own say.
A rubber chicken squeaks with pride,
As cornered cats try to hide.

Time machines in cardboard costumes,
Zooming past all the dusty blooms.
A yoyo flies with reckless glee,
Whispering sarcasm, 'You're stuck with me!'

Old photographs with silly grins,
Peeking through the laughter thin.
Each snapshot holds a giggling past,
A snapshot of craziness unsurpassed.

So let's rewind and play pretend,
With socks that don't have a matching friend.
The heart beats funny, loud, and true,
In lives we live, all askew.

Where Stories Begin

Underneath a toadstool bright,
A frog tells tales with delight.
Of knights who'd trip on their own feet,
And fairies dancing to a funky beat.

A grumpy cat sings to the moon,
While squirrels play a jazzy tune.
All the trees nod in a sway,
As books whisper, 'Come out to play!'

Pinecones gather for a chat,
Critiquing the squirrels' funky hat.
In this land of oddities fine,
Everyone joins the merry line.

So let's embark on this quirky quest,
With laughter filling our hearts at best.
Where stories spin, and smiles take flight,
In the silliest grooves of the night!

Pathways of Understanding

In the garden where ideas sprout,
A banana peel's a slip, no doubt.
Laughter echoes through the trees,
Wisdom hidden under leaves.

Worms conduct the earth's decree,
Negotiating with every bee.
They wiggle and dance in cosmic fun,
Turning muck into the sun.

Roots may tangle, trip and dive,
Yet in the chaos, thoughts arrive.
What seems lost becomes a path,
With jokes that make us share a laugh.

So let's dig down, explore the dirt,
Find the humor in the hurt.
With every laugh, we grow more wise,
In this garden of surprise!

Underlying Narratives

Once a seed decided to scold,
'Why do leaves turn red and gold?'
The roots replied with a chuckle,
'It's fall fashion, no need to buckle!'

In the soil, secrets wrap,
As critters plot and take a nap.
They whisper truths, both shy and bold,
With stories that never grow old.

A clump of dirt starts a debate,
On why the sun is always late.
'It's stuck in traffic on rayway nine!'
With each punchline, roots intertwine.

Underneath the surface thick,
Life's a comedy, take your pick!
With humor bound in every layer,
Who knew soil could be the player?

Shadows of Growth

Beneath the darkness, sprouts arise,
Whispering jokes in low disguise.
Each shadow hides a pun or two,
And giggles echo in the dew.

Roots do the cha-cha in the black,
Twisting, turning—never lack.
They tickle weeds with every push,
In this wacky underground rush.

One day a sprout dared to say,
'Is it just me, or is it gay?'
The roots all chuckled, a wink in tow,
Together in this veggies' show.

As sunlight beams through leafy hats,
They throw a bash for all the gnats.
In shadows deep where laughter grows,
The roots plant joy—everyone knows!

Nature's Secret Story

In a garden where giggles grow,
The daisies dance, putting on a show.
Worms wear glasses to read the sun,
And ants prank butterflies just for fun.

The rain chuckles as it starts to drip,
While squirrels on branches do a little flip.
Bees are buzzing a sweet little tune,
As daisies gossip with the morning moon.

Tendrils of Life

Little shoots stretch up to the sky,
With dreams of reaching clouds way up high.
A snail in a race just to prove it's fast,
Shouts, "I'll win this time, at last!"

Fungi hold parties under the trees,
Inviting beetles and buzzing bees.
And roots tell tales in whispers low,
Of adventures wherever they go.

Currents of Heritage

In a stream where the fish like to jest,
They wear tiny hats and play at best.
A frog with a crown hops on a log,
Singing to crickets, his royal cog.

Tadpoles dream of becoming grand,
While turtles do yoga on the sand.
The water flows with laughter and cheer,
As dragonflies spin with no hint of fear.

The Hidden Mosaic

A patchwork quilt of leaves and laughter,
Where every stitch hides a tale, you'll see after.
A chipmunk in socks waltzes in style,
While vines crack jokes to make you smile.

Petals wear hats made of raindrop pearls,
Swirling around as the breeze twirls.
And beneath the surface in dirt so fine,
Tiny critters raise a glass of sweet wine.

Shadows of the Past

In a sock drawer, where dreams go to fade,
Old memories gather, a curious parade.
Mismatched socks whisper of wild, youthful nights,
Underneath piles of dust, they plot their delights.

Forgotten toys giggle in their wooden beds,
While dust bunnies dance; lightening choking threads.
Cursed by the closet, the secrets they hold,
Are worth more than gold, or so they're all told.

Lifting the Veil

Under the kitchen sink, I found a surprise,
A grin from a sponge and a rogue rubber fry.
Together they plotted a bubble-rup game,
While the blender snorted, calling them lame.

With a flick of the switch, chaos did reign,
As forks and spoons gathered, to dance on the rain.
A spatula spun tales of pancakes in flight,
While the kettle laughed, brewing giggles at night.

Cracks in the Surface

On sidewalks where secrets lay buried so deep,
Cracks in the pavement keep watch, never sleep.
They chuckle at footsteps, the journeys they bring,
Like gossiping grandmas that chortle and sing.

With every new bump, a new tale is spun,
Of skateboard adventures, or races just won.
Those cracks roll their eyes at the weight of our woes,
As they stretch in the sun, where no one quite goes.

The Soil Speaks

If you listen close, the garden will chat,
About veggies' ambitions and how to grow fat.
Tomatoes brag loudly of red, juicy fame,
While carrots, in modesty, play their own game.

Worms throw a rave under old cabbage leaves,
While beetles debate who's the best of the thieves.
With laughter and muck, they keep roots all aglow,
In a world where the soil knows just where to go.

Underlying Currents

Life's a dance beneath the ground,
With twinkle toes, roots twirl around.
They're late for tea, but bring a snack,
And giggle as they never look back.

Plant a joke and watch it sprout,
With puns so punny, you'll laugh out loud.
The underground's a comedy scene,
Where worms wear wigs and beetles preen.

They whisper tales of soil's delight,
As moles and gophers have their fight.
Organic humor flows and swells,
While dandelions ring their bells.

So raise a cup of muddy cheer,
Toast to roots that thrive down here!
For laughter is what makes us grow,
In this zany garden show!

The Web of Existence

Spiders spinning giggly threads,
Connecting life from toes to heads.
Each silly strand, a funny link,
Where frogs discuss their dreams in pink.

Mice in tuxedos dance with grace,
While ants in line have a cheeky race.
A party here, with snacks galore,
Even leaves join in and explore!

Corona of kookiness today,
We're intertwined in a silly way.
Chasing tails, and getting lost,
In this web, what's the cost?

A tickle here, a giggle there,
Connections made with joyful flare.
So spin your yarn, weave your line,
For life's a joke, oh so divine!

Seeds of the Present

Tiny seeds in pockets hide,
With dreams too big, they laugh and bide.
Plant me here, call me what you wish,
I'll just sprout into a slushy dish!

Sunflower hats on ladies fair,
Grow wild ideas for all to share.
The daisies tease the butterflies,
While carrots joke about "no fries."

A sprinkle here, a chuckle there,
With every bloom, we play and dare.
Life's a salad of humor fine,
Tossed with dressing, oh how we shine!

So gather round and plant a laugh,
Each seed will sprout a shining path.
For in this garden where we play,
Comedy's the star of the day!

Ancestral Echoes

From roots of yore, the giggles grow,
Whispering voices in winds that blow.
"Don't eat yellow snow!" they chime,
In echo chambers of ancient rhyme.

Great-grandpa grinning with cheeky eyes,
Telling tales that make us sigh.
"Did I ever tell you 'bout the shoe?"
The family legend: tall but true!

A recipe for laughter shared,
Absurdity's what we all have bared.
So dance along these paths of cheer,
With echoes ringing, crystal clear.

For every giggle and every grin,
The past connects us deep within.
So cherish humor from days of old,
In every story, let joy be told!

Where Life Takes Hold

In the garden, gnomes look wise,
Counting raindrops from the skies.
Worms do disco in the dirt,
Pants all muddy, oh, what a flirt!

Seedlings dance with newfound flair,
Tickled by the gentle air.
Roots like fingers stretch and reach,
Learning life's extended speech.

Chickens gossip with the coons,
Plotting parties 'neath the moons.
Sunflowers nod at every joke,
While cabbage rolls out the cloak.

Laughter swirls in leafy shades,
As tangled tales of life cascades.
In this plot where humor grows,
Joyful chaos, who knows?

Silent Testimonies

Beneath the roots, a secretive chat,
Between the fungi and the old hat.
They're gossiping about the leaves,
Who knew trees could be such thieves?

A squirrel's stash of nuts so grand,
Buried deep in someone's land.
Each acorn holds a tale of wit,
As laughter echoes where they sit.

Branches bending, reaching wide,
Mice in boots take a wild ride.
Rabbits chuckle, "What a sight!,"
While owls hoot with pure delight.

In silence, all the whispers bloom,
In emerald vistas, life finds room.
And in the shadows, stories mold,
Unseen laughter—silent, bold.

Interwoven Pathways

Roots entangle like a dance,
Twisting, turning, not a chance.
Tiny critters join the fun,
Underneath the warming sun.

Beneath the soil, a bustling spree,
A secret party, oh so free!
Dance partners made of twig and leaf,
In joy, they find sweet relief.

Worms with hats, they grooved along,
To the rhythm of the tree's song.
Every tangle tells a joke,
In this club, all roots provoke.

Through laughter shared, they find their way,
In every twist, the games they play.
Messy networks, vibrant trails,
Echoed joy in all their tales.

Cradle of Aspirations

In a pot, a plant dreams high,
Wishing for clouds in the sky.
Sprouting thoughts of where to go,
Maybe to that garden show!

A bean sprout plans a daring leap,
"I'll reach the stars while others sleep!"
Buds debating upon their fate,
"Hop on board, let's navigate!"

Grass blades whisper plans of zest,
Comfy roots, they know the best.
A tumbleweed with wanderlust,
Rolling tales is a must!

In this cradle, hopes entwine,
Laughter serves as their design.
In every dream that takes its flight,
They plot adventures, day and night.

Legacy of Moments

In a garden of giggles, we plant our seeds,
Watering memories, pulling a few weeds.
The laughter we sow, like sunshine in spring,
Flourishing smiles, oh, what joy they bring!

From socks left behind, to the pie that got burned,
In shared little moments, our hearts have discerned.
Every slip and every trip, turns into a cheer,
Add some sprinkles of fun, they're golden memories here!

With each clumsy adventure, we cherish the fun,
Like a race with no winners, just joy for everyone.
Our stories unfold, in a comical dance,
Tickled by times when we dared to take chance!

So let's toast to the moments, frail yet so bright,
With chuckles and grins, we'll savor the night.
For in the tall tales, and whispers of fate,
We gather the laughter, our own cherished state.

Crossroads of Time

At the intersection where clocks go to play,
We stumble and fumble, in our wobbly way.
Yesterday's tacos still linger around,
But future burritos are waiting, abound!

On this path lined with chuckles and dreams,
We chase after llamas while bursting at seams.
Time flies like squirrels, darting across roads,
But joy lingers longer than heavy loads!

With signs that say 'Detour' and 'Turn Back,'
We navigate nonsense, keeping on track.
Each glance in the rearview is filled with delight,
As laughter echoes softly, into the night.

So here's to the crossroads, both wild and sublime,
Where quirky collides with the rhythm of time.
We dance to the tick-tock, in all of its rhyme,
For the silliest moments are truly the prime.

The Unseen Network

Behind every chuckle, a thread's tightly spun,
Connecting our stories, in webs of pure fun.
With laughter as currency, we trade and we share,
In this zany exchange, we haven't a care!

Like squirrels with secrets, we plot and we scheme,
Creating connections that spark and that gleam.
Through hidden encounters, we giggle and play,
In this vast silly circuit, we'd never delay!

The puns float like bubbles, we chase without end,
In this whimsical network, we gather, we blend.
Each chuckle's a spark, igniting the day,
Together in nonsense, we dance and we sway!

So here's to the fibers that weave through the air,
Binding us tightly with laughter to share.
In this unseen network, we comically thrive,
For in humor and bliss, we are truly alive!

Footprints Beneath Us

In the sand of our antics, we leave silly tracks,
Like footprints of marshmallows and tiny knick-knacks.
Every laugh is a step, every joke is a leap,
We skip through the chaos, no time for a sleep!

Our shoes are mismatched, but who really cares?
We dance on the shores of whimsical dares.
With every ridiculous twist and odd turn,
Our paths light up bright, as for giggles we yearn!

We follow each other down paths yet unseen,
With trails made of nonsense, and bursts of bright green.
Every stumble a story, every slip an embrace,
In this funny adventure, we find our own space!

So let's run through the sprinklers, barefoot and bold,
With footprints that dazzle, in stories retold.
For in laughter's warm glow, we chase what we seek,
In the footprints beneath us, our hearts play
hide-and-seek!

Veins of Creation

In a garden where laughter thrives,
Seeds of chaos play and jive.
Beneath the soil, dreams sprout wide,
Worms wearing glasses, full of pride.

On the edge of whimsy's shore,
Ideas float, they dance and soar.
What's that sapling? A joke it tells,
With roots that tickle, how it dwells!

Funky flowers hum a tune,
Bongo beats beneath the moon.
Nature's giggle shakes the ground,
In this wild, we're joy unbound.

Laughter echoes through the trees,
Squirrels juggling with such ease.
From nutty puns to acorn quips,
Life's crack-up with comic flips.

Threads of Connection

In a web of jokes and jest,
Laughter binds us, we're the best.
With each pun, a thread is spun,
Knitted harmony, oh what fun!

Through tangled vines of silly tales,
We share our hearts, like laughing whales.
Banana peels on golden days,
Slip into giggles, in so many ways.

The more we joke, the more we cheer,
Connections grow, less doubt, less fear.
Like a sock that's lost, a friend returns,
In laughter's glow, a heart that learns.

With every smile, a knot unties,
Woven joys, oh how time flies!
Threads of humor crisscross tight,
Turning gray skies into pure light.

Birthplaces of Wisdom

In the cradle of giggles, wisdom begins,
Where puns come to life, and humor wins.
With quirky thoughts and wacky lore,
We learn to laugh and then explore.

Old trees wear hats made of yarn,
Whispering secrets, causing charm.
Sage advice from a playful crow,
"Always bring snacks when you go!"

Down in the soil of quirky dreams,
Knowledge sprouts with silliness beams.
Each thought a stepping stone so bright,
In the garden of laughter, pure delight!

Funkiness grows in every nook,
Each wise crack, like a storybook.
Explore the brain where giggles abide,
In the land of chuckles, joy won't hide.

Hidden Intersections

In alleyways where giggles hide,
Two paths cross in joyful stride.
Banana skins and spaghetti swirls,
At this junction, laughter twirls.

Three old dogs share a story,
Of how they chased the mailman's glory.
Their tails wagging in grand delight,
Under the sun, everything feels right.

The traffic of jokes flows so free,
Where punchlines collide, just wait and see.
Mishaps weave a colorful thread,
In this maze, we giggle instead.

Laughter lanes lined with cheer,
In each twist, we lose our fear.
Finding joy in every crack,
At hidden intersections, there's no lack.

Foundations of the Unseen

In the basement, dust bunnies play,
Finding treasures from yesterday.
Forgotten socks join in a dance,
Their partner? A cheese wheel in a trance.

Underneath, the spiders weave,
A tapestry of tricks, you wouldn't believe.
They throw a party, no one knows,
Even the mice are dressed in clothes!

A rat with a hat and a monocle too,
Sips on tea, invites the zoo.
Chairs made of boxes, a couch of old rags,
They laugh at the cat, such a source of gags!

So next time you sweep, take care, take heed,
For down there, they gather, a very fun breed.
With laughter and joy, like a silly play,
The unseen foundation is where they stay.

Echoes of the Ancients

In caves where shadows dance and prance,
Old echoes tell tales of a wild romance.
A caveman slips on a bone that's slick,
He lands with a thud, what a comical trick!

Pictographs show mammoths in capes,
Laughing while dodging those odd stone shapes.
An ancient shaman with paint in his hair,
Sings to the stars, but forgets how to share!

With firelight flickers and shadows that creep,
The owls all hoot, losing count of their sheep.
They giggle and hoot, a prehistoric laugh,
While the caveman grunts, "Just forget the math!"

So when you think back to days long past,
Remember they smiled, and their diets were vast.
They chanted and danced, in funny old ways,
Creating the echoes that still fill our days.

Ties that Bind

A shoe lace unties just when you run,
Tangled together, oh what fun!
The cat gets involved, thinking it's prey,
While you trip and tumble, then laugh it away.

Friendships are like that, a knot or two,
Sometimes they tangle, make life feel like glue.
But when you untie, and laugh at the mess,
You find all the joy in the funny excess.

Shared pies, shared fries, and secrets in gasps,
Laughter that bubbles, through giggles and clasps.
A bond that weaves through thick and through thin,
Binding us close, through each silly grin.

So cherish those ties, the odd, and the loose,
For in every mishap, there's a reason to truce.
And when it breaks down, and causes some fright,
Just laugh at the chaos, it will turn out alright!

Beneath the Bark

Under the bark, the squirrels convene,
Planning their heists, clever and keen.
With acorns in hand, they strategize well,
A nutty conspiracy, they giggle and yell!

Raccoons drop by, with masks on their face,
Stealing from trees, oh what a race!
Rooting and tooting, they dance all around,
Spreading the tales of what they found.

A turtle remarks, 'It's a secretive game,
Where everyone's welcome, still no one's to blame.'
But beneath their fun, there's wisdom galore,
Nature's own laughter, a comical lore.

So next time you wander near trees that you see,
Listen real close, you might hear the spree.
For beneath the bark, wild parties ignite,
With laughter and joy, into the night!

Deep Waters of Life

In the ocean's embrace, fish learn to dance,
Dancing like noodles, they take a chance.
A crab with a hat, what a sight to see,
Sipping a cocktail, laughing in glee.

Seahorses tiptoe, like they're at a ball,
Wiggling their tails, trying not to fall.
Jellyfish float by, with style and grace,
But one takes a tumble—oh, what a face!

A whale sings a tune, it's offbeat and loud,
As fish form a conga, all wriggly and proud.
In deep waters, surprises await in a whirl,
Life's a grand ocean; just give it a swirl!

So come dive with laughter into these deep seas,
Where even a clam can tickle your knees.
With bubbles and giggles, it's all quite a sight,
In waters of joy, everything feels right.

Cradled in the Earth

In the soil so soft, worms wiggle with cheer,
Cheering for daisies, their favorite dear.
A gopher pops up, adjusting his tie,
As ants march in line, oh my, oh my!

Rocks hold a party, they clink and they clatter,
"Did you hear the gossip?" said a stone—"What a chatter!"
The roots share their secrets, while twirling around,
Whispering jokes that make the soil sound.

The daffodils chuckle at a passing breeze,
While over in shadows, the fungi tease.
"Hey, look at us! We're having a ball!"
In the earth's cozy arms, life's a great haul!

So cradle yourself, let the laughter take flight,
In the muck and the mire, it's a pure delight.
For in this great dirt, where wonders are found,
Life giggles and wiggles, all happily bound.

Nature's Heartbeat

In the babbling brook, frogs croak a tune,
Hopping on lily pads, beneath the full moon.
A squirrel with style, in shades and a hat,
Squeaks out a jingle, "Isn't life fat?"

Bees buzz in rhythm, making sweet gold,
While butterflies dance, oh, so bold!
A raccoon in slippers is stealing some pie,
With a wink and a grin, he says, "Oh, me, why?"

The trees sway and whisper, they've tales to tell,
Of acorns with dreams, and seedling wishes swell.
They giggle in tandem with the rustling leaves,
As the wind tells the story that nature weaves.

So laugh with the crickets, let your spirit take flight,
In nature's grand symphony, it's sheer delight.
For every heartbeat, every chuckle unfurls,
It's a party among the petals and pearls!

Where Stories Emerge

In the forest's embrace, shadows begin,
A hungry raccoon finds his way to a bin.
"Look at this treasure!" he squeals with a laugh,
As he wears a doughnut like a hilarious scarf!

Trees stand like giants, with eyes full of glee,
Gossiping branches sway, "Did you hear about me?"
A woodpecker knocks, trying to stay relevant,
He taps on the trunk with such bold accident!

In the twilight's glow, a firefly choir sings,
With the crickets and frogs, oh, the joy that it brings!
As tales intertwine, quietly they merge,
In this great dance of life, where stories emerge.

So come share your laughter, beneath the stars so bright,
For even the shadows have stories tonight.
In every twinkle of stars, find a funny old fable,
Nature's own script, like a whimsical fable!

From Ashes to Hope

From the ash, a seed takes flight,
Wiggling worms bring dreams to light.
A dandelion's crown, a queen's delight,
In muddy puddles, frogs recite.

With chuckles bright, we plant the day,
Giggling seeds in a funny way.
Each sprout a joke that loves to play,
Nature's humor on display!

In sunlit patches, laughter blooms,
As squirrels dance, defying gloom.
Beneath the trees, in joyful rooms,
Life's punchlines echo, fun resumes.

From chaos born, a garden grows,
With roots in laughter, nobody knows.
We build it up with silly prose,
A patchwork plot, funny woes.

Branches of Narratives

Twisted tales on branches sway,
Where pigeons gossip every day.
A squirrel's stunt, a feathery ballet,
The shade's a stage for the fray.

Leaves gossip in whispered tones,
Casting shadows on ancient bones.
Pine cones drop with silly thrones,
As nature jests in funny tones.

In the breeze, stories unfold,
Of woodpeckers, brave and bold.
Each crack of bark, a joke retold,
And trees stand watch, a sight to behold.

Roots digging deep beneath the jest,
Where laughter lives and never rests.
A tapestry formed from whimsy's zest,
Chronicles found, hilarity blessed.

Harvesting Histories

In fields of giggles, surprises grow,
Where the sunflowers steal the show.
Pumpkins chuckle, all aglow,
As corn stalks nod in a row.

With baskets full of ripe delight,
We skip and dance, hearts light.
Tomatoes wear coats of red so bright,
In this harvest, nothing's contrite.

Carrots joke with leafy greens,
In patchwork plots of droll machines.
Radishes burst in laughter's sheen,
As nature's jesters form a scene.

In pots of gold, we store our fun,
Each veggie's tale, under the sun.
With every bite, the joy is spun,
Harvesting giggles, everyone!

Conduits of Change

Rivers chuckle as they flow,
Tickling banks where wildflowers grow.
A fish's leap steals the show,
As breezes whisper tales we know.

Mountains grin with rocky smiles,
Echoing laughter for miles and miles.
Each pebble tells of funny trials,
Pathways twist with whimsical styles.

With every step, the earth will tease,
Shaking leaves, swaying trees.
A parade of ants in funny fees,
Marching forth with nimble ease.

In every nook, a giggle waits,
In weathered signs and creaky gates.
Where change is fun, and life creates,
A world of jokes that never abates.

Deep in the Earth

Deep down below, where the worms like to play,
Riddles of mud, they think they can sway.
But little do they know, it's all in good fun,
The laughter of soil, when the day's finally done.

Fossils cracked jokes in the old dusty caves,
Tickling each other like playful young knaves.
They giggle and wiggle in sediment's glee,
While roots spin tall tales as they sip their sweet tea.

Beneath all our feet, a party takes place,
Where rocks like to dance at their own rugged pace.
They're throwing a bash, with a dew drop or two,
Celebrating life's quirks, as they play peekaboo.

So next time you stroll on the ground that you tread,
Remember the antics of what lies ahead.
The underground antics, they're quite a delight,
In the epic of nature, it's a comical sight!

The Fabric of Being

Woven with laughter, the threads intertwine,
Each stitch a story, over coffee and wine.
The fabric of nonsense, it stretches so wide,
With jokes about socks that take life in stride.

A tapestry blooms, where backgrounds all clash,
The colors are zany, like a clown's loud splash.
Every fabric heart beats in rhythm so crazy,
Making all of existence feel mildly hazy.

So grab your own needle and stitch with a grin,
Don't worry too much about where to begin.
With every wild fiber, a chuckle you'll score,
Life's quilt is a riot, who could ask for more?

Laughter's the warp that holds us all tight,
In this hilarious weave, everything feels right.
Stitch after stitch, our tales will unfold,
In comedy's warmth, we've got pure gold!

Birthplaces of Thought

In cafes where ideas find freedom to roam,
A coffee spill turns to a thought's new home.
Napkins are scribbled with dreams and with schemes,
As laughter erupts from the wildest of memes.

Eureka! They shout, when a bright thought appears,
Like confetti on birthdays, it sparkles with cheers.
They ponder and ponder, in circles they roam,
Until someone yells, "Let's just grab a cone!"

In corners they giggle, ideas intertwine,
A brainstorm that's messy, like ketchup and brine.
With quirky inventions that boggle the mind,
Creativity's playground is where we'll unwind.

So raise up your glass, toast to the bizarre,
Where laughter and genius hang out, near and far.
In the birthplaces of thought, we embrace the absurd,
Turning whimsy to wisdom, without saying a word!

Connections in the Dark

In the dark of the night, where shadows play neat,
Whispers of friendships echo down every street.
With laughter like fireflies, they flicker and dance,
Creating connections that'd make you take a chance.

Under the moon, where the wackiest meet,
Jokes travel faster than light on their feet.
They share secret giggles and tales that are bright,
Turning awkwardness into sheer comic delight.

The stars startickling as night draws its cloak,
While chortles and chuckles slip into a joke.
With each punchline flung, a bond stronger grows,
In this nightly cabaret, anything goes!

So if you find yourself out in the night,
With the creatures of laughter that fill up your sight,
Join the loops of fun, let your worries depart,
In this wild connection, we all share a heart!

The Language of Roots

In a garden deep and wide,
The veggies chat, no need to hide.
They gossip low beneath the dirt,
"Did you hear? That lettuce flirt!"

The carrots chuckle, roots all tangled,
While radishes dance, a bitangled.
Turnips play poker, well-established,
In a world where potatoes are lavish---

A crow drops by, says, "What on earth?"
"You folks are weird, but full of mirth!"
They laugh and say, with leafy flair,
"You can't get this fun from fresh air!"

Cracks of laughter sprout and bloon,
As flowers jive beneath the moon.
Roots may burrow, shy and meek,
But they speak volumes—though not a squeak!

Innocence in the Soil

Underneath the shady trees,
Worms play tag, the silliest tease.
"You missed me!" squeaks the little one,
Then giggles echo, oh what fun!

A daisy blushes, root-bound shy,
"Can you not see? I'm quite spry!"
But coming close, you'd hear them scream,
Nature's children, lost in a dream.

The beetles race in tiny cars,
They drive in circles, fueled by stars.
And clovers chat without a care,
"Don't pull my leaves! That's just not fair!"

When rain clouds dance, the soil bursts,
Jumping in puddles, quenched from thirsts.
Innocence found, in dirt they play,
Smiles bloom brighter than the day!

Veils of Memory

In the roots where old tales dwell,
They whisper secrets, oh so swell.
"I remember when I was a sprout!"
One claims boldly, with roots to tout.

The pebbles giggle, sparked with mirth,
"Oh, tell us more, of your time on earth!"
A sage old stump shares wisdom grand,
"There was a time, I ruled this land!"

The ferns roll their eyes and snicker loud,
"You were just a twig, surrounded by proud!"
But every root has tales to weave,
In the soil where dreams never leave.

Memory dances on the breeze,
Carried by ants with utmost ease.
With laughter growing through the ground,
Life's funny moments all around.

The Foundation of Thought

In the mud where ideas grow,
A brainstorm blooms, putting on a show.
The sprouts debate their next big scheme,
"Let's be broccoli!" or so it seems.

Through tangled thoughts, the daisies muse,
"Should we wear hats? Or just refuse?"
While sunflowers nod, basking in sun,
"Whatever we pick, let's have some fun!"

A cantaloupe shouts, "Hey, wait, hold on!"
"I'm ripe for the picking, let's now respond!"
The radishes blush, a hit or a miss,
In the garden of minds, who could resist?

Ideas sprout, with laughter's spark,
Roots of nonsense, leaving their mark.
Foundation built on giggles and glee,
In the soil of jest, where we're all free!

Ties that Bind Us.

In the tangled web of life, we find,
Connections made, often unwrapped and blind.
A sock lost here, a shoe stuck there,
We laugh at the chaos, stuck in mid-air.

A spaghetti strand ties us to a plate,
While silly string jokes never seem to abate.
We trip on our ties, then break into cheer,
Life's a big knot, but we hold it dear.

From family to friends, our bonds do stretch,
Like elastic bands, not easy to fetch.
So let's tie it together, in giggles and grins,
Life's silly fabric, where the fun never thins.

With every new twist, the laughter will flow,
In this comedy act, we'll steal every show.
For through all the laughter, the jokes keep us tight,
In the great grand design, we dance in delight.

Whispers of Beginnings

In the dawn of time, a tiny seed spoke,
Yet no one heard—except for a joke.
It whispered softly to the nearby breeze,
'I'm just a sprout, but I'll make you wheeze!'

With each little poke from the warm early sun,
New sprouts emerged, claiming laughter's fun.
A dance of green whispers in the refreshing air,
'We're just starting out, but hey—who cares?'

The roots tickle ground, 'Is this where we grow?'
While worms wiggled in, putting on a show.
Every giggle surfaces, from soil to sky,
Beginnings are funny, oh my, oh my!

So here's to new starts, where odd things collide,
Let the whispers of beginnings be our joyful guide.
Through quirks and through turns, we flourish and sprout,

In this whimsical dance, let laughter burst out!

Under the Surface We Grow

Beneath the topsoil, in shades of grime,
Roots wiggle and squirm, like it's all part of time.
They gossip and giggle, these tangled odd twigs,
Plotting their moves like mischievous digs.

They've heard the old tales of plants high and proud,
So down in the dirt, they converse, oh so loud!
'Stomping humans up there seem so sure,
But we know the secrets; we're the real cure!

With tendrils like fingers, they tickle the earth,
In this underground party, there's plenty of mirth.
Seeds roll their eyes at the plants up above,
'Just wait 'til we bloom, it'll be a wild love!'

So here's to the roots, those jokers unseen,
Crafting a world filled with laughter between.
In the quirk of the soil, comedy flows,
For beneath all the laughter, a true garden grows.

Seedlings of Existence

A tiny little seed cracked out of its coat,
Wobbled and wiggled, trying to gloat.
'Look at me sprout, I can do a jig!
I'm the cutest of plants, don't you wanna dig?'

With sunshine above, and water below,
They started to strut in a green little show.
'Just give us some soil, and watch us all shine,
This garden of giggles is totally divine!'

Each leaf a performer, each thorn a good jest,
Silly seedlings dance, they feel truly blessed.
A chorus of laughter fills the warm summer air,
As petals join in, skipping without a care.

From small sprigs to strong, they grow and they play,
In this garden of wonder, they brighten the day.
For in every seed, lies a laugh yet untold,
A quirky existence, just waiting to unfold.

Echoes of Ancestry

Great-uncle Joe wore socks with flair,
Dancing like he just didn't care.
A family tree of oddball kin,
Watch us tangle, laugh, and spin!

Auntie Sue bakes cakes, oh what a sight,
With secret herbs that feel just right.
Cousins giggle, sugar in hand,
In this madcap, quirky clan!

Grandpa's tales are quite the hoot,
Of how he fought a chicken, to boot!
We gather 'round, all ears and glee,
To hear the saga of the family tree.

So raise your glass to those who came,
In a legacy that's wild and untamed.
With laughter echoing through the years,
We celebrate our roots with cheers!

Foundations of the Mind

In the attic lies a box of dreams,
Filled with odd thoughts and wild schemes.
A paper hat, a rubber duck,
Who knew a mind could be so stuck?

A cousin's question, 'Why the sun?'
Answers tangled—oh, it's just fun.
Spinning theories, we zoom and race,
Like a hamster on a wheel in space!

Grandma thinks that aliens tease,
They swap our socks while we just sneeze.
Logic giggles behind the wall,
As we ponder it all, and have a ball!

So here we are, with thoughts so grand,
Building castles in this merry land.
With laughter guiding where we roam,
Foundations made, we call it home!

A Tangle of Beginnings

Twisted vines, a web of fate,
Brought together by a quirk so great.
Uncle Fred's hat, a wondrous sight,
Makes him look like a festive kite!

Sister's giggles as she pranks the cat,
While Dad dons Grandma's huge old hat.
From odd traditions, we choose to grow,
A blend of chaos in every show!

A recipe for laughter, a dash of fun,
Cooking with cousins—what have we begun?
Spaghetti flying, and sauce on the wall,
It's just dinner, no big deal at all!

Yet in every mishap, there's love to find,
Crafted by mishaps, forever entwined.
So we laugh as we weave our stories tight,
In this tangled dance of sheer delight!

From Soil to Soul

Digging deep in the garden bed,
Finding treasures and things we said.
Worms are wriggling, putting on a show,
While daisies dance, and sunflowers glow!

Mom's advice: 'Just grow and thrive,'
As we water dreams, feel so alive.
Pickles from cucumbers, oh what a treat,
In this vibrant patch, life's bittersweet!

A scarecrow stands with a goofy grin,
Guarding veggies, the battle's begin!
Yet how they mingle, soil meets heart,
Turning this garden into a work of art!

So here we cultivate joy and cheer,
From humble dirt to dreams we steer.
With laughter sprouting in every row,
Our quirky family continues to grow!

Awakening the Understory

In the soil's warm embrace, they wiggle and dance,
Little critters and fungi, oh what a chance!
Twirling and whirling beneath our feet,
Making the world taste fresh and sweet.

They gossip with roots, share secrets in glee,
Who would have thought? Not you or me!
A family reunion where nobody's seen,
Creating connections, if you know what I mean!

Worms tell the tales of the nutrients lost,
While moles keep it tight, round the underground host.
Every little beetle on their merry way,
Ensuring the flora gets its buffet.

So giggle a bit as you walk through the green,
For the party below is a riotous scene!
Who knew that the roots had such a fun side?
Digging for laughs, they bury their pride!

Soil of Being

Nestled deep down, where the sun seldom shines,
A world full of chatter, secret sign lines.
Hilarious microbes, they juggle and jest,
In a soil sandwich, they're having the best!

Caterpillars lounge on a leaf's comfy seat,
Sharing wild tales of their treats and their feats.
As they munch on the mallow, oh what a sight,
Life in the dirt is a whimsical delight!

The roots don't just cling; they tell jokes and puns,
Playing tag with the bits that make up our buns.
The soil's a stage where all creatures perform,
Join in the laughter, let chaos conform!

So while you're above, don't forget what you miss,
Underground antics can lead to pure bliss.
So lift up a cup, let's toast to the ground,
Where humor thrives, and joy can be found!

A Symphony of Connections

Beneath our shoes, there's a concert unplanned,
Roots strumming notes with a mischievous hand.
The fungi are singing, the worms tap their feet,
It's a classic performance that's hard to beat!

A chorus of laughter, a harmonized hum,
As beetles join in, they shake their teeny drum.
The air is all lifted, it dances with glee,
Who knew that the dirt held a jubilee?

So as you stroll by, don't silence the cheer,
For the soil is alive, and it wants you near.
Step lightly and listen; let nature confide,
There's a show in the muck that's too grand to hide!

With every soft rustle, a punchline unfolds,
Uncover the humor that the earth gently holds.
These roots aren't just anchors, they're comedians too,
Laughing beneath us, all dressed up in dew!

Discoveries Below

What treasures lie deep in the underworld's lair?
A hoard of hilarity, beyond all compare!
With roots like detectives, they're piecing the clues,
Each worm offers wisdom on what to peruse.

A tangle of stories, a riotous quest,
As they play hide and seek, these roots know best.
Each little tickle from a bug or a sprout,
Makes for a narrative worth raving about!

Down in the depths, the giggles do grow,
In a riveting race against what we think we know.
So take a deep breath as you dig into life,
There's humor in dirt, no reason for strife!

When you peek underground, let your worries unbind,
For the fun never stops in the depths you can find.
With roots as your friends, and soil as your guide,
Dive into the laughter; let curiosity ride!

www.ingramcontent.com/pod-product-compliance
Lightning Source LLC
Chambersburg PA
CBHW072220070526
44585CB00015B/1428